Nita Mehta's
Dal & Roti

Prepare your Dal differently, instead of the old boring routine!

Nita Mehta

B.Sc. (Home Science), M.Sc. (Food and Nutrition), Gold Medalist

SNAB
Publishers Pvt Ltd

Nita Mehta's
Dal & Roti

© Copyright 1995-2008 **SNAB** Publishers Pvt Ltd

15th Print 2008
ISBN 978-81-86004-06-7

Food Styling and Photography: **SNAB**

Layout and laser typesetting :

National Information Technology Academy
N.I.T.A. 3A/3, Asaf Ali Road
☎ 23252948 New Delhi-110002

Contributing Writers :
Anurag Mehta
Subhash Mehta

Editorial & Proofreading :
Rakesh
Ramesh

Distributed by :

THE VARIETY BOOK DEPOT
A.V.G. Bhavan, M 3 Con Circus,
New Delhi - 110 001
Tel : 23417175, 23412567; Fax : 23415335
Email: varietybookdepot@rediffmail.com

Printed by :

Paras Offset Pvt. Ltd., C-176, Naraina, Phase-1 New Delhi-28

Published by :

SNAB
Publishers Pvt. Ltd.
3A/3 Asaf Ali Road,
New Delhi - 110002
Tel: 23252948, 23250091
Telefax:91-11-23250091

Editorial and Marketing office:
E-159, Greater Kailash-II, N.Delhi-48
Fax: 91-11-29225218, 29229558
Tel: 91-11-29214011, 29218727, 29218574
E-Mail: nitamehta@email.com
snab@snabindia.com
*Website:*http://www.nitamehta.com
Website: http://www.snabindia.com

Rs. 89/-

Nita Mehta's **BEST SELLERS (Vegetarian)**

All Time Favourite SNACKS

CHAAWAL

Desserts & Puddings

Green Vegetables

Food for Children

Low Calorie Recipes

Microwave Cookery

The Art of BAKING

NAVRATRI
NO ONION NO GARLIC

Soups Salads & Starters

South Indian

Vegetarian Dishes

With love to my dear mother
Suniti Kshetrapal
who taught me the basics of cooking.

CONTENTS

ROTI   81
Cooking Tips for Roti   82

INTRODUCTION

In every Indian home, dal is eaten at least once a day. For the vegetarians, it's the main source of proteins. The nutritive value of dals can be greatly enhanced by the addition of vegetables like spinach, mushrooms, ghiya, carrots, raw mango or chopped coconut. Besides increasing the nutritive value, these vegetables give variety to the dals. Sprouting of dals, increases their digestibility and nutritive value. There is an appreciable increase in the B vitamins and 80-100 fold increase in the vitamin C content.

Indian names for various ingredients have been used for convenience. However, their English equivalents are also given in brackets along with the Indian names.

Here's to healthy cooking with dals and rotis!

Nita Mehta

INDIAN NAMES	ENGLISH NAMES
Aam	Mango
Ajwain	Thymol seeds, Carom seeds
Amchoor	Dried mango powder
Anardana	Pomegranate seeds
Arhar ki dal	Red gram
Atta	Whole wheat flour
Besan	Gram flour
Channe ki dal	Split gram
Dalchini	Cinnamon
Dhania	Coriander
Dhania saboot	Coriander seeds
Garam masala	Mixed spices
Haldi	Turmeric
Hing	Asafoetida

INDIAN NAMES	ENGLISH NAMES
Imli	Tamarind
Jeera	Cumin seeds
Kabuli channe	Bengal gram
Kali mirch	Black pepper
Kali mirch saboot	Pepper corns
Kalonji	Nigella seeds, Onion seeds
Kasoori methi	Dry fenugreek leaves
Laung	Cloves
Lehson	Garlic
Maida	Plain flour
Masoor ki dal	Lentil
Matar	Peas
Methi dana	Fenugreek seeds

INDIAN NAMES	ENGLISH NAMES
Mooli	Radish
Dhuli Moong ki dal	Split green beans
Moong Saboot	Green beans
Moti illaichi	Brown cardamom
Nariyal	Coconut
Nariyal ka burada	Desiccated coconut
Palak	Spinach
Poodina	Mint leaves
Rai	Fine mustard seeds
Saunf	Aniseed
Tej patta	Bay leaf
Til	Sesame seeds
Urad dhuli	Split black beans
Urad saboot	Whole black beans

COOKING TIPS FOR DALS

- Soak whole pulses (saboot dals) overnight or soak in boiling water for 20 minutes, to soften skin.
- Split or dehusked pulses (dhuli dals) can be soaked in cold water for half an hour before cooking.
- Use the same water for cooking in which pulses have been soaked.
- Add a few drops of oil or ghee during cooking to reduce the cooking time and frothing.
- Do not use cooking soda as it destroys the vitamin B content.
- If 1 cup dal is to be cooked, add 3-4 cups water to it, depending on the type of dal.
- Well cooked & blended dals taste better.

Baghar or Tempering

Indian style of serving dals is with a baghar. Baghar adds to the flavour of the dal and also sparks the look.

Jeera-Dhania Baghar

Servings 4

INGREDIENTS

3-4 tbsp ghee or oil
½ tsp jeera (cumin seeds)
½ tsp garam masala (mixed spices)
½ tsp dhania (coriander) powder
1/8 tsp amchoor (dried mango pd.)
½ tsp red chilli powder
2 tbsp chopped coriander leaves

METHOD

1. Heat oil or ghee in a pan. Reduce flame.
2. Add jeera. Fry till seeds turn golden brown. Do not burn them.
3. Add dhania powder, amchoor and garam masala. Cook for ½ minute.
4. Remove from fire and add red chilli powder and coriander leaves. Mix well for 2-3 seconds.
5. Pour over the hot cooked dal. Mix gently.

TOMATO - ONION BAGHAR

Servings 4

INGREDIENTS

3-4 tbsp ghee or oil
½ tsp jeera (cumin seeds)
1 onion - chopped finely
1 tomato - chopped finely
1 green chilli - slit length ways into four pieces
½ tsp garam masala (mixed spices)
½ tsp dhania (coriander) powder
1/8 tsp amchoor (dried mango powder)
½ tsp red chilli powder

Arhar with Palak : Page 22, Nans :. Page 110

METHOD

1. Heat oil or ghee; reduce heat. Add jeera. When it turns golden, add onions.
2. Cook till onions turn brown. Do not under cook the onions. Brown them, stirring continuously.
3. Add tomatoes. Cook for 2-3 minutes on low flame.
4. Add dhania powder, amchoor and garam masala. Cook for ½ minute.
5. Remove from fire. Add the green chillies and red chilli powder. Mix well.
6. Pour over the hot dal. Mix gently.

Hing - Sarson Baghar

Servings 4

INGREDIENTS

3-4 tbsp oil
1/8 tsp hing (asafoetida powder)
¼ tsp sarson (mustard seeds)
2 whole dry red chillies
a few curry leaves

METHOD

1. Heat oil; reduce heat. Fry hing powder till brown.
2. Add mustard seeds. Fry till they crackle.
3. Remove from fire. Add red chillies and curry leaves.
4. Mix well. Add to the hot cooked dal.

Dals

For a family of 4, normally 1 cup dal is enough. Saboot (whole) dals take longer to cook and hence more water, about 5 cups of water to 1 cup uncooked dal are added. For dhuli (dehusked) dals, add 3 cups of water to 1 cup uncooked dal. Dals may be boiled in a handi or a pateela, though pressure cooking is faster.

Picture on page 17

ARHAR WITH PALAK

Serves 4

INGREDIENTS

3 cups (250 gm) chopped palak (spinach)
1 cup arhar dal or toovar ki dal (red gram dal)
1 small clove garlic - finely chopped (optional)
½ " piece ginger - finely chopped
1 green chilli - finely chopped
½ tsp haldi (turmeric powder)
1½ tsp salt - to taste
1 tsp oil
tomato - onion baghar - page 16

METHOD

1. Pick, clean and wash dal. Wash chopped palak in plenty of water.
2. Mix dal, palak, garlic, ginger, green chilli, haldi, salt and oil. Add 3 cups water to the dal.
3. Pressure cook dal to give one whistle & then keep on low flame for 6-7 minutes. Remove from fire.
4. Prepare tomato-onion baghar as given on page 16 & pour over the hot dal. Mix gently. Serve hot.

MOONG DAL WITH WADI

Serves 4

INGREDIENTS

1 cup dhuli moong dal (split green beans)
1 wadi
1 tomato - cut into big pieces
1" piece ginger - grated
2 tbsp oil
½ tsp haldi (turmeric powder)
1½ tsp salt
Jeera - dhania baghar - page 14

METHOD

1. Fry the wadi in oil, on low flame; turning sides, till it turns golden brown. Cool and break it into 3-4 pieces.
2. Pick, clean and wash dal.
3. Add 3½ cups water, salt, haldi, ginger, tomato, fried wadi and the left over oil in which the wadi was fried.
4. Pressure cook to give one whistle. Remove from fire immediately.
5. Prepare jeera-dhania baghar as given on page 14 and pour over the hot cooked dal. Mix gently. Serve hot.

Picture on page 52

MASOOR DAL WITH VEGETABLES

Serves 4

INGREDIENTS

1 cup malka masoor dal (lentil)
1 onion - cut into rings
1 carrot
¼ of a small cauliflower
2-3 laung (cloves)
2 tbsp oil
1½ tsp salt
½ tsp haldi
3 cups water
2 tsp lemon juice
jeera dhania baghar - page 16

26

METHOD

1. Cut cauliflower and carrot into ½" pieces. Heat oil in a pressure cooker. Add onions. Fry till light brown.
2. Add vegetables and laung. Cook for 2-3 minutes.
3. Add washed dal. Add salt, haldi and 3 cups water and pressure cook to give one whistle. Remove from fire immediately.
4. Prepare jeera dhania baghar as given on page 14 & pour over the hot dal.
5. Add lemon juice to dal. Mix. Serve hot.

CHANNE KI DAL WITH GHIYA

Serves 4

INGREDIENTS

1 cup channe ki dal (split gram)
½ small (200 gms) ghiya (bottle gourd) - peeled & chopped
1½ tsp salt
½ tsp haldi (turmeric powder)
2 tsp desi ghee or oil
½ tsp red chilli powder
tomato-onion baghar - page 16

METHOD

1. Pick, clean and wash dal.
2. Mix dal, ghiya, salt, haldi, desi ghee, red chilli powder and 4 cups water in a pressure cooker.
3. Pressure cook for 5 minutes on low flame after the first whistle. Remove from fire.
4. Prepare tomato-onion baghar as given on page 16 and pour over the hot cooked dal. Mix gently. Serve hot.

KHATTI DAL

Serves 4

INGREDIENTS

1 cup malka masoor (lentil)
½ of a lemon sized ball of imli (tamarind)
½ tsp haldi
1½ tsp salt
tomato-onion baghar - page 16

METHOD

1. Pick, clean & wash dal.
2. Add 3 cups water, haldi & salt.
3. Pressure cook to give one whistle. Remove from fire immediately.
4. Soak imli in hot water for 5-7 minutes. Squeeze to extract pulp.
5. Prepare tomato-onion baghar as given on page 16.
6. Pour the imli extract into the baghar after it is ready. Boil.
7. Pour the baghar into the hot dal. Mix. Serve hot with rice.

MOTH

Serves 4

INGREDIENTS

1 cup moth (brown beans)
1½ tsp salt
½ " stick dalchini (cinnamon)
2 laung (cloves)
2 moti illaichi (big cardamoms)
4 saboot kali mirch (pepper corns)
½ tsp haldi (turmeric powder)
1" piece ginger - crushed to a paste
3-4 flakes garlic - crushed to a paste
tomato-onion baghar page 16

METHOD

1. Soak moth in boiling water for 10 minutes to soften the skin.
2. Grind ginger and garlic to a paste.
3. Pressure cook moth, dalchini, laung, seeds of moti illaichi, kali mirch, haldi, salt and ginger-garlic paste together. Add 5 cups water.
4. After the first whistle, keep on low flame for 15 minutes. Remove from fire.
5. Prepare tomato-onion baghar and pour over the hot dal. Mix well. Serve hot.

Note : Moong Saboot (whole green beans) can also be prepared in the same way.

FIVE SPICE ARHAR

Serves 4

INGREDIENTS

1 cup arhar dal (red gram dal)
½ tsp haldi (turmeric powder)
1½ tsp salt
1 green chilli - chopped finely
½" piece ginger - grated
3-4 tbsp ghee

FIVE SPICES

2 pinches of methi dana (fenugreek seeds)
¼ tsp sufed jeera (cumin seeds)
¼ tsp black jeera (cumin seeds)

¼ tsp saunf (aniseeds)
1/8 tsp ajwain (thymol seeds)

METHOD

1. Pick, clean and wash dal. Pressure cook dal with salt, haldi, green chilli, ginger and 3 cups water.
2. After the first whistle, keep on low flame for 6-7 minutes. Remove from fire. Keep aside.
3. Heat ghee in big karahi. Reduce heat. Collect all the spices together & add to the hot ghee.
4. Fry the spices on low flame for a few seconds.
5. Pour the hot dal into the five spice baghar. Mix well on fire for a few seconds. Serve hot.

CHANNE KI DAL WITH COCONUT

Serves 4

INGREDIENTS

1 cup channe ki dal (split gram)
½ tsp haldi (turmeric powder)
1½ tsp salt
1 tsp ghee or oil
¼ cup chopped fresh coconut
2 tbsp chopped coriander

BAGHAR

½ tsp jeera (cumin seeds)
1" piece ginger
1 dry red chilli

2-3 tbsp ghee
½ tsp each of garam masala & dhania (coriander) powder

METHOD

1. Clean & wash dal. Add haldi, salt, 1 tsp oil or ghee and 3 cups water. Pressure cook to give on whistle. Keep on low flame for 5-6 minutes. Remove from fire.
2. For the baghar, grind ginger & dry red chilli to a paste.
3. Heat ghee in a karahi. Add jeera. When it turns golden, add ginger paste. Cook for a few seconds only.
4. Add garam masala & dhania pd. Cook for ½ minute.
5. Add the boiled dal to the baghar. Add coconut also. Boil.
6. Remove from fire and serve hot garnished with coriander.

MUGLAI DAL

Serves 6

INGREDIENTS

1½ cups dhuli urad dal (split black beans)
3½ cups water
1 tsp haldi (turmeric powder)
100 gms paneer (cottage cheese) - cut into cubes & fried
1 tsp black pepper
2 green chillies - finely chopped
2 tbsp chopped coriander leaves
½ tsp jeera (cumin seeds)
2 tsp chopped ginger
1 small onion - finely chopped

1 medium firm tomato - finely chopped without pulp
4 tbsp ghee or oil
salt to taste
¼ cup cream

METHOD

1. Soak urad dal for one hour.
2. Boil water with haldi and salt.
3. Add soaked urad dal, fried paneer and cook till the dal becomes tender and each grain is separate.
4. Now put dal in a strainer so that excess water may be removed. Keep aside.
5. Fry finely chopped onion in ghee till it turns light brown. Add finely chopped ginger, and fry till onion turns golden brown.

6. Add jeera and fry for a second and mix with the dal.
7. Add finely chopped green chillies and coriander leaves to the dal.
8. At the time of serving put the dal in a dish and sprinkle chopped tomato without pulp and then pour the cream over it.

PANCHRATNI DAL

Serves 4

INGREDIENTS

3 tbsp urad dhuli dal (split black beans)
3 tbsp arhar dal (red gram dal)
3 tbsp channe ki dal (split gram)
3 tbsp moong dhuli dal (split green beans)
3 tbsp saboot masoor dal (lentil)

BAGHAR
3 tbsp oil
1 tsp rai (mustard seeds)
1 tsp jeera (cumin seeds)
2 laung (cloves)

½" stick dalchini (cinnamon)
few curry leaves
2 dry red chillies - broken into bits
2 green chillies - chopped
½" ginger piece - chopped
3 tomatoes - chopped
½ tsp garam masala (mixed spices)
1 tbsp of chopped coriander
juice of ½ lemon

METHOD

1. Clean, wash all dals. Pressure cook together with 3½ cups of water and 1½ tsp of salt.
2. After the first whistle, keep on low flame for 5-7 minutes. Remove from fire. Keep aside.

3. Collect mustard seeds, jeera, dalchini and laung together.
4. Heat oil. Reduce heat. Add the collected jeera etc. Cook for a few seconds. Add ginger, curry leaves, red and green chillies. Fry for a few seconds.
5. Add the tomatoes and garam masala and cook for 1-2 minutes. Add this baghar to the dal. Add coriander also.
6. Bring dal to boil, keep on slow fire for 2-3 minutes.
7. Add lemon juice. Mix well. Serve hot.

SAMBHAR

Serves 4

INGREDIENTS
---

1 cup mixed vegetables - mooli (radish), onion, potato,
bhindi (ladies finger), brinjal, capsicum - cut into ½ " pieces
2 green chillies - slit lengthways
½ cup arhar dal (red gram)
3 tsp sambhar powder
½ teaspoon haldi (turmeric powder)
1 tbsp rice flour - optional
lemon-sized ball of imli (tamarind)
salt to taste
1 small bunch chopped coriander leaves for garnishing

BAGHAR
2 tbsp oil
½ tsp sarson (mustard seeds)
¼ tsp hing (asafoetida) powder
¼ tsp methi dana (fenugreek seeds)
½ tsp jeera (cumin seeds)
1 dry red chilli, a few curry leaves

METHOD

1. Pressure cook dal with 2 cups of water till well blended.
2. Soak imli in 1 cup of hot water and extract pulp.
3. Heat oil. Add all the ingredients of the baghar. When the mustard seeds splutter, add the slit green chillies and the chopped vegetables. Fry for 3-4 minutes.
4. Add the imli pulp, salt, haldi and sambhar powder. Cover and simmer on a low heat till the vegetables are tender.

5. Add the cooked dal and simmer for 5 minutes till everything blends.
6. If the sambhar needs to be thickened, make a smooth paste of the rice flour in 2 tbsp of water and add to the sambhar and cook for another 2-3 minutes, till the raw smell disappears.
7. Garnish with chopped coriander leaves. Serve hot with rice.

Rasam

Serves 4

INGREDIENTS

2 tomatoes - cubed
¼ tsp hing (asafoetida) powder
2 tsp rasam powder - page 49
¼ cup arhar dal (red gram)
lemon-sized ball of imli (tamarind)
salt to taste
chopped coriander leaves for garnishing

BAGHAR
2 tsp oil

1 tsp jeera (cumin seeds)
1 red chilli, a few curry leaves

METHOD

1. Pressure cook dal with 1½ cups water for 15 minutes after the first whistle. The dal should be soft and well blended.
2. Boil imli in water and extract pulp.
3. Mix tomatoes, imli extract, hing powder, rasam powder and salt in a pan. Add 1 cup water. Simmer for about 15 minutes.
4. Add the cooked dal and enough water to get a thin watery rasam. Boil for 10-15 minutes. Keep aside.
5. Heat 2 tsp oil and add all the ingredients for baghar. When the mustard seeds splutter, add to the rasam. Garnish with chopped coriander leaves. Serve hot.

Rasam Powder

2½ cups saboot dhania (coriander seeds)
1¼ cups red chillies
½ cup saboot kali mirch (pepper corns)
3/4 cup arhar (red gram) dal
¼ cup channe ki dal (Bengal gram dal)
½ tbsp jeera (cumin seeds)
1 tsp haldi (turmeric)
1 small bunch curry leaves

1. Roast all dry ingredients separately, except haldi. Mix all ingredients together and grind to a fine powder.
2. Store in an air-tight container and use as required.

DAL PALAK
Serves 4

INGREDIENTS

½ cup channe ki dal (split gram)
½ kg palak (spinach)
2 tomatoes
1-2 green chillies - chopped
½ " piece ginger - chopped
1 tsp dhania (coriander) powder
½ tsp garam masala (mixed spices)
½ tsp red chilli powder
3 tbsp oil
1 onion - chopped

Dal with Capsicum & Mushrooms : Page 65

METHOD

1. Soak dal for ½ hour.
2. Wash, chop palak leaves. Discard the stems.
3. Heat oil in a pressure cooker. Fry onions till golden brown.
4. Strain the soaked dal. Add dal, palak and all other ingredients, including the spices into the pressure cooker.
5. Cook for 1 minute. Add ¼ cup water.
6. Pressure cook to give 2 whistles, then cook on low heat for 8-10 minutes.
7. After the pressure comes down, mash the dal slightly.
8. Serve hot with boiled rice or rotis.

DAL MAHARANI

Serves 4

INGREDIENTS

1 cup urad dhuli dal (split black beans) - soaked for ½ hour
1" piece ginger - very finely chopped
4-5 flakes garlic (optional) - very finely chopped
2 green chillies - very finely chopped
½ tsp haldi (turmeric) powder
1¼ tsp salt
1 cup water

BAGHAR
1 big onion - finely chopped

1 big tomato - finely chopped
½ mooli (radish) with tender leaves
chopped leaves of one radish (5-6 leaves)
½ tsp garam masala (mixed spices)
½ tsp chilli powder
3-4 tbsp ghee or oil

METHOD

1. Clean, wash dal. Soak dal in water for ½ hour. Strain dal.
2. Pressure cook dal with 1 cup water and all the other ingredients. When the first whistle comes, slow down the fire & keep for 1 minute only.
3. Remove from fire. Open the cooker only after the pressure drops down. Keep aside.
4. Cut radish leaves into thin long strips.

5. Heat ghee. Add onions. Cook till brown. Add tomatoes. Cook for 2-3 minutes.
6. Add chopped radish. Cook for 1 minute.
7. Add radish leaves. Mix. Add ½ tsp chilli powder and ½ tsp garam masala. Cook for ½ minute.
8. Pour over the dal. Mix gently. Serve hot.

DAL MAKHANI

Serves 6

INGREDIENTS

1 cup urad saboot (whole black beans)
2 tbsp channe ki dal (split gram dal)
2 tbsp rajmah (kidney beans) - soaked for 5-6 hours, optional
1 tbsp ghee or oil
5 cups of water
1½ tsp salt
1" piece ginger
4 flakes garlic (optional)
2 dry red chillies
3 tomatoes - pureed in a grinder
¼ cup beaten curd

½ cup cream
3 tbsp ghee or oil
2 tsp dhania (coriander) powder
½ tsp garam masala (mixed spices)
¼ tsp grated jaiphal (nutmeg)
1 tbsp butter

METHOD

1. Grind ginger, garlic & dry red chillies together to a paste.
2. Clean, wash dals. Pressure cook both dals and the soaked rajmah with 1 tbsp ghee, water, salt and half of the ginger-garlic paste. Keep the left over paste aside.
3. After the first whistle, keep on low flame for 40 minutes. Remove from fire. Keep aside.
4. Heat ghee. Add tomato pureed in a grinder. Cook until ghee separates and it turns thick.

5. Add curd. Cook until ghee separates and it turns red again.
6. Add the left over ginger paste, garam masala & coriander pd. Cook for a few seconds. Add this tomato mixture to the boiled dal. Add butter.
7. Simmer on slow fire for 8-10 minutes, stirring occasionally.
8. Add cream and jaiphal. Remove from fire. Serve hot.

Quick Rajmah Curry

Servings 4

INGREDIENTS

1½ cups lal rajmah (red kidney beans) - soaked overnight
1 tbsp channe ki dal (split gram) - soaked overnight
2 tsp salt or to taste
1 onion - chopped finely
6-8 flakes garlic - crushed, 1" piece ginger - chopped finely
4 tbsp oil
3 tomatoes - pureed in a blender
½ cup curd - beaten well
3 tsp dhania powder, ¼ tsp amchoor
½ tsp garam masala, ½ tsp chilli powder (or to taste)
2 tbsp chopped coriander, 2 laung (cloves) - crushed

1. Pressure cook rajmah, channe ki dal, salt, chopped onion, garlic and ginger together with enough water to give one whistle. Keep on low flame for ½ hour. Remove from fire.
2. Heat 4 tbsp oil in a heavy bottomed kadhai. Add tomatoes pureed in a blender. Cook till tomatoes turn dry.
3. Reduce flame and add dhania powder, garam masala, red chilli powder & amchoor. Cook till oil separates.
4. Add beaten curd and stir continuously on low flame till the masala turns red again and oil separates.
5. Add powdered laung.
6. Strain & add the rajmahs, keeping the water aside. Stir fry on low flame for 5-7 minutes, mashing occasionally.
7. Add the water of the rajmahs and pressure cook again for 8-10 minutes on low flame after the first whistle.
8. Remove from fire. Garnish with freshly chopped coriander leaves. Serve hot with chappatis or boiled rice.

Picture on inside front cover

PUNJABI CHHOLE

Serves 4

INGREDIENTS

PRESSURE COOK TOGETHER
1 cup channa kabuli (Bengal gram)
2 tbsp channe ki dal (split gram)
2 moti illaichi (big cardamoms)
1" stick dalchini (cinnamon)
2 tsp tea leaves tied in a muslin cloth or 2 tea bags

MASALA
3 onions - chopped finely
1½ tsp anaardana (pomegranate seeds) powder
3 tomatoes - chopped finely

1" piece ginger - chopped finely
1 green chilli - chopped finely
½ tsp garam masala
2 tsp dhania powder
2 tsp channa masala
salt & red chilli powder to taste

METHOD

1. Soak channa and channe ki dal overnight or for 6-8 hours in a pressure cooker. Next morning, discard water. Wash channas with fresh water and add moti illaichi, dalchini, tea leaves, ¼ tsp soda and enough water to cover the channas nicely.

2. Pressure cook all the ingredients together to give one whistle. After the first whistle, keep on low flame for about 20-25 minutes. Keep aside.

3. Heat 4 tbsp oil. Add onions. Saute till transparent. Add anaardana powder. Cook stirring till onions turn golden brown. (Do not burn them).
4. Add chopped tomatoes, ginger and green chill. Stir fry for 3-4 minutes.
5. Add dhania powder, chilli powder and garam masala. Mash and stir fry tomatoes occasionally till they turn brownish in colour and oil separates.
6. Strain channas, reserving the liquid. Remove tea bag from the boiled channas and add to the onion-tomato masala. Mix well. Add salt. Stir fry gently for 5-7 minutes.
7. Add channa masala and salt. Add the channa liquid. Cook for 15-20 minutes on medium heat till the liquid dries up a little.
8. Serve garnished with onion rings, green chillies and tomato wedges.

DAL WITH CAPSICUM-MUSHROOMS

Serves 4

INGREDIENTS

1 cup channe ki dal (split gram)
½ tsp haldi (turmeric powder)
1½ tsp salt
2 tsp ghee
3-4 laung (cloves)
1 tej patta (bay leaf)

BAGHAR
3 tbsp oil
1 onion - chopped finely
1 tomato - chopped finely

50 gms (1 cup) mushrooms - chopped
1 big capsicum - chopped finely
½ " piece ginger
2 flakes garlic - optional
½ tsp red chilli powder
½ tsp garam masala (mixed spices)
1 tsp dhania (coriander) powder

METHOD

1. Pick, clean and wash dal.
2. Add haldi, salt, laung, tej patta, ghee & 4 cups of water.
3. Pressure cook to give one whistle. Keep on low flame for 8 minutes.
4. Grind ginger & garlic to a paste.
5. Heat oil. Add onion. Cook till brown. Add tomatoes.

Cook for 2-3 minutes on low flame. Add dhania powder and garam masala. Cook for ½ minute.

6. Add mushrooms. Cook for 3-4 minutes on low flame till they get cooked.

7. Add ginger-garlic paste and capsicum. Cook for ½ minute. Remove from fire.

8. Add the boiled dal. Mix well. Serve hot.

Sweet and Sour Moth

Serves 4

INGREDIENTS

1 cup month (brown beans)
½ tsp haldi (turmeric powder)
1" stick dalchini (cinnarnon)
2-3 moti illaichi (brown cardamom)
a lemon sized ball of imli (tamarind)
5-10 gms (a very tiny piece) of gur (jaggery)
½ tsp jeera (cumin seeds)
1 tsp saboot dhania (coriander seeds)
1 green chilli
½" piece ginger

1 onion - finely chopped
1 tbsp oil
1 tej patta (bay leaf)
1 tsp red chilli powder
½ tsp garam masala (mixed spices)
1 tbsp chopped coriander

METHOD

1. Boil moth with salt, haldi, dalchini, moti illaichi and enough water.
2. Wash and boil imli in some water. Squeeze and extract pulp.
3. Roast jeera and dhania together on a tawa.
4. Grind dhania, jeera, ginger and green chilli to a paste.
5. Heat oil. Add onion. Cook till transparent.

6. Add tej patta and the paste. Cook for ½ minute.
7. Add imli extract and gur. Boil.
8. Add the boiled moth.
9. Add red chilli powder, garam masala and salt to taste.
10. Serve sprinkled with chopped coriander.

Masala Masoor

Serves 4

INGREDIENTS

1 cup saboot masoor (lentil)
1 big onion - sliced finely
2 large tomatoes - chopped
4-6 small whole onions
2 tbsp ghee
1½ tbsp chopped coriander

PASTE

4 cloves garlic
2 dry red chillies
2 tsp dhania saboot (coriander seeds)
1 tsp jeera (cumin seeds)
1½ " piece ginger

METHOD

1. Pick, clean and wash masoor.
2. Add 5 cups water and the whole onions.
3. Pressure cook for 10-12 minutes on low flame after the first whistle. Keep aside.
4. Grind all ingredients of the paste together.
5. Heat ghee in a karahi. Add sliced onions. Fry for 3-4 minutes till they turn brown.
6. Add paste to the onions. Cook for 2-3 minutes on low flame.
7. Add the cooked masoor and salt. Keep on slow fire for 5 minutes.
8. Add tomatoes. Cook for 10 minutes.
9. Serve hot, sprinkled with chopped coriander.

SHAJAHANI DAL

Serves 8

INGREDIENTS

250 gm kabuli peas - soaked for 8-10 hours
3 onions - finely chopped
2 green chillies - finely chopped
1 tsp red chilli powder
1 tsp garam masala (mixed spices)
1 tsp dhania (coriander) powder
2½ tsp salt
6 laung (cloves)
2 small sticks dalchini (cinnamon)
4 chhoti illaichi
1 small coconut

2 cups milk
3 tbsp ghee
2 tbsp chopped coriander

METHOD

1. Grate coconut. Add 1 cup hot water & keep aside for 10-15 minutes. Squeeze well to extract coconut milk.
2. Boil 2 cups of milk, till it is reduced to ½ cup.
3. Scrub the soaked peas with the hands to remove the thin white skin.
4. Pressure cook peas with extra water till soft.
5. Blend the peas to a dal like paste.
6. Heat ghee. Add chopped onions. Cook till transparent.
7. Crush laung, dalchini and seeds of chhoti illaichi. Add to the cooked onions. Cook for 1 minute.

8. Add salt, red chilli powder, dhania powder, garam masala and green chillies. Cook for ½ minute.
9. Add dal. Mix. Boil.
10. Add coconut milk and ½ cup of thickened milk. Cook for 2-3 minutes.
11. Add chopped coriander and cook till thick. Serve hot.

Picture on page 18

SUKHI URAD DAL

Serves 4

INGREDIENTS

1 cup dhuli urad (split black beans) - soaked for 20 minutes
1 tbsp oil
½ tsp haldi
1¼ tsp salt
½ tsp jeera (cumin seeds)
¼ tsp garam masala (mixed spices)
¼ tsp dhania (coriander) powder
¼ tsp red chilli powder

BAGHAR
3 tbsp oil
1 onion - sliced finely
¼ tsp red chilli powder
1 tsp shredded ginger
1 tbsp chopped coriander

METHOD

1. Strain the soaked dal & keep aside.
2. Heat 1 tbsp oil in a pressure cooker. Add jeera.
3. When it turns golden, add the dal.
4. Add salt, haldi, garam masala, red chilli powder & dhania powder.
5. Stir on low flame for 1 minute.
6. Add 1 cup water.

7. Pressure cook to give one whistle. Keep on low flame for 1 minute only. Remove from fire immediately.
8. Heat 3 tbsp oil in a small pan. Add onions & cook till they turn brown. Remove from fire.
9. Add chilli pd. Pour the baghar over the dal. Mix gently.
10. Serve hot garnished with shredded ginger and chopped coriander.

KASOORI METHI WITH DAL

Serves 4

INGREDIENTS

½ cup moong dhuli (split green beans)
½ cup masoor dhuli (lentil)
2 tbsp kasoori methi (dry fenugreek leaves)
½" piece ginger - grated, 1 dry red chilli
1 tsp oil
1½ tsp salt
½ tsp haldi (turmeric powder)

BAGHAR
3-4 tbsp oil
a pinch of hing (asafoetida)

¼ tsp methi dane (fenugreek seeds)
½ tsp each of garam masala (mixed spices), dhania powder
½ tsp red chilli pd.

METHOD

1. Pick, clean & wash both dals together. Add kasoori methi, ginger, oil, 1 dry red chilli, salt and haldi to dal.
2. Pressure cook dals with 3½ cups water to give one whistle. Actually the fire can be shut off when the whistle just starts. This dal gets over cooked in one whistle also, at times.
3. Heat oil in a small pan. Add hing. Cook for ½ minute.
4. Remove from fire. Add methi dana. Cook on low flame till it turns golden. Add red chillies, dhania & garam masala. Cook for a few seconds. Pour over the hot dal.

Roti

Roti eaten with Dal is a valuable source of proteins as different proteins supplement each other. Whole grain cereals like atta, are rich in iron, vitamin B and fibre. Refined cereals like maida, however, furnish very little of these nutrients.

COOKING TIPS FOR RO TI

- Knead dough well and keep it covered for half an hour before using, to allow gluten strands to develop. If this is not done, its puffing quality is affected and the edges become cracked.

- Use appropriate amount of water to make the dough so that it does not become too dry or too wet in cooking. Cereals have different hydration capacity.

  For example, atta needs about 60 percent water (by weight) to form a soft dough for chapaties and paranthas.

- Add less water for making a firm dough for poories and kachories.

- Do not use too much dry flour in rolling the dough.
- Use a heavy griddle for cooking chapaties and paranthas.
- Heat ghee to smoking point before frying poories.

CHAPATI OR PHULKA

Serves 4

INGREDIENTS

2 cups atta (whole wheat flour)
½ cup water - approx.
2 tsp ghee - optional

METHOD

1. Sift atta into a flat basin (parat). Make a depression in the centre of the heap and add some water. Mix. Add the remaining water gradually, kneading to a smooth and soft dough.
2. Cover the dough with a wet cloth for about 30 minutes.

3. Knead the dough again for 5 minutes.
4. Make balls, slightly smaller than the size of a lemon.
5. Heat the tawa (griddle) on fire.
6. Roll balls into fairly thin rounds about 5-6" in diameter.
7. Place the chapati on the hot griddle and reduce the flame. Cook the chapati on moderate heat throughout.
8. Turn over when tiny bubbles appear on the surface. Cook till brown spots are formed on the under surface.
9. Turn over and press lightly on the sides with a folded cloth till the chapati is puffed or bloated. Do not puff directly on flame.
10. Remove from tawa. Apply ghee on one side.
11. Serve immediately or keep them wrapped in a clean cloth in an air tight box.

MISSI-ROTI

Serves 4

INGREDIENTS

1 cup besan (gram flour)
1 cup atta (whole wheat flour)
2 tbsp oil or melted ghee
1 tbsp kasoori methi (dry fenugreek leaves)
½ tsp salt
½ tsp red chilli pd.
½ tsp jeera (cumin seeds)
a pinch of hing (asafoetida)
a pinch of haldi (turmeric powder)

METHOD

1. Mix all ingredients. Add enough water to make a dough of rolling consistency.
2. Cover it and keep aside for ½ hour.
3. Make 6 balls.
4. Roll each ball into a chapati, but thicker than the usual chapati.
5. Cook on a hot tawa by frying it or in a hot tandoor.
6. When made in a tandoor, apply ghee and serve immediately.

GOBHI PARANTHA

Makes 4

INGREDIENTS

2 cups whole wheat flour (atta)
½ tsp salt
about ¾ cups water to knead

FILLING

2 cups grated cauliflower
1 tsp salt
½ tsp garam masala
½ tsp red chilli powder
1" piece ginger - grated finely
2-3 tbsp chopped, fresh coriander, oil or butter for frying

METHOD

1. Mix salt and whole wheat flour. Add enough water to get a dough or rolling consistency. Knead well till smooth. Cover and keep aside for at least 30 minutes.
2. For filling, add all ingredients to the grated cauliflower and mix well. Keep aside for 15 minutes. Squeeze the cauliflower well after 15 minutes to drain out the excess water.
3. Make 2 marble sized balls of the dough. Roll out each ball into very thin rounds. Spread some filling on one and cover with the other round. Press the edges well to join.
4. Carefully pick up the parantha and put it on a hot tawa (griddle). When the underside is cooked, turn to cook the other side. Smear some oil or butter on the parantha. Trickle some oil on the sides too, around the edges. Turn and brown both sides. Similarly make other paranthas.
5. Serve with plain yogurt and some pickle or chutney.

TANDOORI ROTI

Serves 4

INGREDIENTS

2½ cups atta
1 cup water (approx.)
½ tsp salt
2-3 tbsp ghee

METHOD

1. Keep ghee in the fridge for some time, so that it solidifies.
2. Make a soft dough with atta, salt and water. Keep aside for half an hour.
3. Divide the dough into 6 equal balls. Flatten each ball, roll out each into a round of 5" diameter.

4. Spread 1 tsp of solidified ghee.
5. Make a slit, starting from the centre till any one end.
6. Start rolling from the slit, to form an even cone. Roll out, to a diameter of 5", applying pressure only at the centre.
7. Cook carefully in a heated tandoor.

Note : An old cooker or a big dalda tin to which a handle is attached, can be conveniently used in a place of a tandoor. Clean the cooker or the gas tandoor well. Smear some oil on the sides. Then wipe it well with a clean napkin. Apply some water on the roti, stick on the sides of the cooker or tandoor. In case the roti falls on to the gas, it means there is excess oil on the sides of the cooker or tandoor; or too little water is applied on the roti before sticking it. If it is a problem to take out the roti from the cooker or tandoor, then oil the cooker or tandoor once again.

ALOO WALI TANDOORI ROTI

Serves 4

INGREDIENTS

2½ cup atta (whole wheat flour)
½ tsp salt
2 tbsp oil
½ tsp red chilli pd.

FILLING
2 potatoes - boiled and mashed
1 onion - finely chopped
1 green chilli - finely chopped
salt to taste
½ tsp amchoor (dried mango pd.)

½ tsp red chilli pd.
½ tsp garam masala (mixed spices)

METHOD

1. Mix atta, oil, salt & red chilli pd. Knead with enough water to a soft dough of rolling consistency. Keep aside.
2. Mix all ingredients of the filling.
3. Make a small thick chapati of the dough.
4. Spread a thin layer of the filling all over the chapati.
5. Cut a slit from one end of the chapati till the centre.
6. Start rolling from the slit to form a cone.
7. Press the cone gently from the top.
8. Roll out. Stick in a hot tandoor by applying water on the back side of the chapati.
9. Serve hot, smeared with a little ghee.

ORDINARY PARANTHA

Serves 4

INGREDIENTS

2½ cup atta (wholewheat flour)
½ tsp salt
3-4 tbsp ghee

METHOD

1. Sift the flour and add a little salt and 2 tsp ghee.
2. Rub the ingredients with the fingers to mix them thoroughly.
3. Pour a little water at a time and knead to a soft but not a very soft dough.

94

4. Take small portions of the dough, roll them out into chapatis and smear with ghee.
5. Fold into half, then again into half to form a triangle. Roll out once more to a big triangle.
6. Put one parantha at a time on a heavy and hot tawa (griddle), cook one side and turn over.
7. Add a little ghee from the sides till it gets a nice brown colour.
8. Cook on a low flame and when ready it should be crisp.
9. Similarly, make more paranthas.

BESAN PARANTHA

Serves 4

INGREDIENTS

2½ cups atta (whole wheat flour)
1¼ cup besan (gram flour)
salt to taste
½ tsp red chilli powder
2 tbsp ghee
1 tsp ajwain
1 tsp chopped green chillies
2 tsp anardana (pomegranate seeds) - crushed

METHOD

1. Sift both the flours. Add 1 tbsp ghee. Knead them together with water into a dough as for chapatis.
2. Mix all the other ingredients with the flours.
3. Make lemon sized balls.
4. Roll out each to a thick round, smear with a little ghee and make a half way cut from the end to the centre. Roll, starting from the slit, to form a cone.
5. Press the cone, dip into dry wheat flour and roll out into a thin round parantha.
6. Cook both sides of the parantha on a hot tawa (griddle) and then fry well with ghee.
7. Fry till golden brown on both sides.

LACHHA POODINA PARANTHA

Makes 6

INGREDIENTS

3 cups atta (whole wheat flour), 3-4 tbsp ghee, ½ tsp salt
3 tbsp poodina - chopped finely, 1 tsp ajwain

METHOD

1. Mix atta with ghee and salt. Sprinkle water and knead well to a non sticky dough. Set aside for 1 hour.
2. Knead again & make 6 big balls, the size of an onion. Roll out each to a diameter of 8", almost as big as the chakla.
3. Spread ghee all over. Sprinkle some dry atta on the ghee.
4. Pleat the chappati lengthwise into one collected strip.
5. Twist this strip.

6. Coil the strip to get a pedha (round flattened ball).
7. Flatten this ball between the palms of the hands or gently roll on the chakla (rolling board) with the belan (rolling pin) without applying too much pressure, to a small thick parantha of about 6" diameter. Sprinkle some poodina and ajwain. Press with the belan lightly.
8. Cook in a tandoor by applying water on the back side of the parantha. If you like you can cook it on a hot tawa also. To cook on a tawa first make both the sides light brown on a hot tawa. Reduce flame and then using ghee fry till rich brown on both sides on low heat. Press the sides and all over the parantha with a spoon while frying to ensure that it gets cooked since the parantha is a little thick.
9. Remove from tawa on to a clean kitchen napkin and press the hot parantha on the cloth from all sides for the layers to open up and turn flaky. Serve hot.

POORIES

Serves 4

INGREDIENTS

2 cups atta (whole wheat flour)
2 tsp ghee
1 tsp salt
oil for frying

METHOD

1. Sift flour and salt together and rub in melted ghee.
2. Knead to a little stiff dough with water and set aside.
3. Divide dough into small balls and roll out the balls into small rounds using little oil.

4. Heat oil, drop the rolled poories gently into it.
5. Press the sides of the poories with a perforated frying spoon and turn. Fry till golden brown. Drain on brown paper.

DAL STUFFED POORIES

1. Soak 2 tbsp urad dal (split black beans) overnight.
2. Pound coarsely and add 1 chopped onion, 1 chopped green chilli, ¼ tsp salt and ¼ tsp red chilli powder.
3. Make small balls of dough as given on page 100 and flatten.
4. Put a portion of prepared stuffing in the centre, fold the dough to cover, reshape into a ball and roll out into a poori.
5. Deep fry.

BESAN POORIES

Mix ¼ cup besan and 3/4 cup atta instead of 1 cup of atta. Proceed as for poories as given on page 100.

BEETROOT POORIES

Wash, and chop and pressure cook ½ of a small beetroot in very little water for 5 minutes. Grind to a paste and use for making dough with atta as in basic recipe for poories on page 100.

PEA POORIES

Boil ½ cup shelled peas. Mash them. Season with salt & spices. Proceed as in dal stuffed poories, substituting peas for urad dal.

METHI WALI POORI OR PARANTHA

Serves 4

INGREDIENTS

2½ cups atta (whole wheat flour)
1½ cups methi (fenugreek leaves) - chopped finely
2 tbsp oil
1 tsp salt
½ tsp red chill powder
½ tsp garam masala (mixed spices)
½ tsp ajwain (omum)

METHOD

1. Chop methi leaves finely. Mix ½ tsp salt and keep aside for 1 hour.
2. Squeeze methi. Wash several times. Squeeze again to remove water.
3. Mix methi with other ingredients.
4. Knead to a dough of rolling consistency with enough water. Keep aside for ½ hour.
5. For paranthas, make balls, roll slightly, spread ghee nicely all over. Fold into half, then again into half to get a triangle.
6. Roll out. Cook on a tawa, fry with a little ghee.
7. If poories are to be made, keep the dough a little stiffer than the parantha dough and deep fry in oil.

Picture on page 52

POODINA KULCHAS

Serves 4

INGREDIENTS

DOUGH
250 gms maida (plain flour)
¼ tsp dry yeast
¼ tsp baking powder
150 ml - (3/4 cup) warm milk
1 tsp salt
1 tsp sugar
1½ tsp oil
1 tbsp curd

FILLING
1 small bunch of poodina (mint) leaves
3/4 tsp ajwain (carom seeds)
3/4 tsp salt
3/4 tsp red chilli pd.
1 big onion - very finely chopped
2 tbsp chopped coriander leaves

METHOD

1. Dissolve yeast in 2-3 tbsp of warm water.
2. Sift maida. Add sugar and salt.
3. Put curd in the centre of the maida and sprinkle baking powder on it. Leave for a few seconds till it starts bubbling.
4. Add oil and the dissolved yeast. Knead with warm milk to

a dough. The dough should neither be too soft nor too stiff. It becomes loose after it is kept away for a few hours.

5. Grease a polythene, brush the dough with oil. Keep the dough in the polythene, cover it with a pan inverted over it. Keep in the sun or a warm place for 3-4 hours.

6. The dough swells. Knead it again. Keep aside.

7. Mix all the ingredients of the filling as given on page 106.

8. Make balls. Roll out to the desired size. Sprinkle filling all over.

9. Press gently with the rolling pin (belan) and then with your fingers.

10. Stick in a heated tandoor by applying water on the back side of the kulcha.

11. Cook till brown spots appear. Serve hot.

BHATURE

Serves 4

INGREDIENTS

250 gms (2 cups) maida (plain flour)
100 gms (1 cup) suji (semolina)
½ tsp soda-bi-carb.
½ tsp salt
1 tsp sugar
½ cup sour curd
oil for deep frying

METHOD

1. Soak suji in water, which is just enough to cover it. Keep aside for 10 minutes.
2. Sift salt, soda and maida. Add sugar, suji and curd.
3. Knead with enough warm water to make a dough of rolling consistency.
4. Knead again with greased hands till the dough is smooth.
5. Brush the dough with oil.
6. Keep the dough in a greased polythene and keep it in a warm place for 3-4 hours.
7. Make 8-10 balls.
8. Roll each ball to an oblong shape, and deep fry in hot oil.

Picture on page 17

NAN

Serves 4

INGREDIENTS

2½ cups (250 gms) maida (plain flour)
½ cup hot milk
½ tsp baking powder
½ cup warm water (approx)
½ tsp salt
1 tsp kalaunji (onion seeds)
or
1 tsp khus-khus (poppy seeds)

METHOD

1. Heat milk and put it in a parat (large pan). Add baking powder to the hot milk. Mix well and keep it like this for 1 minute.
2. Sift maida & salt together. Add maida to the hot milk. Mix.
3. Knead to a soft dough with enough warm water.
4. Keep in a warm place for 3-4 hours.
5. Make 6-8 balls.
6. Roll out each ball to an oblong shape. Sprinkle some kalonji or khus khus. Press with a rolling pin (belan). Pull one side of the nan to give it a pointed end like the shape of the nan.
7. Apply some water on the back side of the nan. Stick in a hot tandoor.
8. Cook till nan is ready.

METHI WALI MAKAI KI ROTI
Serves 4

INGREDIENTS

2 cups makai ka atta (maize flour)
2 cups chopped fresh methi (fenugreek)
1 onion - finely chopped
2 green chillies - chopped
salt to taste
hot water to knead the flour
ghee or oil to fry the roti

METHOD

1. Sieve the flour. Wash, remove the stems and chop methi.
2. Mix the chopped methi in the flour, add salt, chopped onions and green chillies.
3. Knead the flour with hot water. Knead to a smooth dough.
4. Heat the tawa (griddle). Take a ball of the dough.
5. Roll with the help of a polythene as explained on page 114.
6. Put it on the hot griddle and cook on both sides, and fry the roti like parantha.

Makai ki Roti

Serves 4

INGREDIENTS

2 cups makai ka atta (maize flour)
hot water - to knead, ghee for frying

METHOD

1. Sieve the flour. Knead gently with hot water to a soft dough. Do not knead the dough too much in advance.
2. Tear an old polythene bag into two halves. Keep one piece on the chakla (rolling platform). Put one ball of the kneaded dough on the polythene. Cover with the other piece, such that there is a plastic cover above & beneath the ball.
3. Roll carefully to a slightly thick roti. Cook the roti on both sides on a griddle. Add some ghee and fry on low flame.

The Sweet Touch
MITHI ROTI

2 cups atta (wheat flour)
½ cup sugar or gur (jaggery)
3 tsp saunf (aniseeds)
ghee for frying

1. Sieve & knead atta to a smooth dough with water.
2. Roll out a ball of the dough.
3. Spread ghee, 2 tsp sugar & a big pinch of saunf.
4. Make a slit from the edge till the centre, half way.
5. Roll to form a cone. Press the cone from the top.
6. Roll out to a slightly thick chapati. Cook on a hot tawa on both sides. Fry with ghee on both sides.

Nita Mehta's **NEW RELEASES**

Nita Mehta's Special **Non-Vegetarian** Recipes

Nita Mehta's **101** Vegetarian recipes

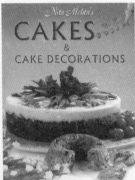

Nita Mehta's **CAKES** & **CAKE DECORATIONS**

Nita Mehta's Special **Vegetarian Recipes**

Nita Mehta's Best of **Indian Cooking**

Nita Mehta's **MEDITERRANEAN** COOKING

Nita Mehta's Cooking for **growing Children**

Nita Mehta's **Zero Oil** Cooking

vegetarian